Sober
Thoughts

A 90 Day Journey for Recovery

Sober Thoughts

SOBER
THOUGHTS

A 90 DAY JOURNEY FOR RECOVERY

Kevin Johnson

HIMPOSSIBLE
PUBLISHING

Copyright © 2022 Kevin Johnson

Scripture taken from the New King James Version®. Copyright© 1982 by Thomas Nelson. Used by permission. All rights reserved.

Printed in the United States of America
26 25 24 23 22   987654321

Publisher: HIMPOSSIBLE Publishing
www.himpossiblepublishing.com
Contact: Himpossible.kj@gmail.com

ISBN: 978-0-578-39858-7
Library of Congress registration: 1-1139063475
Book coach: Rosie Lane Publishing
Cover design: Kendall King- ***kkproductions.biz***
Back cover photo: Jarvis Minton jarvis@blacklabelbrandingco.com
Editor: T.M. Greene

DEDICATION

Now that more than twenty-five years have passed
And the feeling I have; has not been surpassed
So, I take this moment to say, babe, Chocolate chip
You are the only cookie I desire
You are the air that takes me higher
You are the wave that keeps me afloat
You keep me warm like my favorite coat
You are my sunshine
Intoxicating to me like wine
And I'm so glad that you are mine
So, with that being said
And as my heart is led
Thanks for dealing with my imperfections
Thanks for giving me direction
At this time, all I need to say is
I love you more and more each day

Sober Thoughts

ACKNOWLEDGMENTS

First and foremost, I would like to give honor, praise and acknowledgment to my Higher Power who I choose to call God. Through Him All Things are Possible.

I wish to sincerely thank my beautiful wife, Tanya, for her steadfastness through both good times, as well as less than desirable circumstances and situations.

I give thanks to my parents Margaret and Billy Underwood, for giving me the best that they had, of love, guidance and tolerance during my journey from a State of Confusion and despair to the City of Hope and Sobriety. To my grandparents, Nana and Poppa, who were always there.

To my children, grandchildren and great-grandchildren, I pray that you learn from my errors as well as accomplishments so that you could achieve greatness without suffering mistakes with horrible consequences. To my brother, sister, nieces, nephews, uncles and aunts, I pray that my actions, not words make you proud.

To my Pastors, life coaches, counselors and sponsors who provided spiritual uplifting. Thank you for your input during this process. To my dear friends, former and current co-workers, teachers, professors and/or instructors, I appreciate you.

Finally, I wish to thank the naysayers, haters and the devil that drove me closer to my Father, my Lord and Savior, Jesus Christ.

Sober Thoughts

THOUGHTS MATTER!

It has been said, "As a man thinks so is he." When I reached the point of sobriety, my thoughts began to change. I could clearly see the error of my ways and the damage from the mistakes that I had made. I also saw that it was up to me to make the change. Change starts first in the mind. When you change your thoughts you change your life. When you think better, you live better.

Sober Thoughts is a collection of the thoughts from my renewed mind. I don't know all things but experience has taught me many things. I don't focus on regrets from the past because it has passed, but I use the past to push me towards a brighter future. Do I still stumble along the way? Yes, but I don't let that downfall keep me down. My sobriety journey is a work in progress "one day at a time" and one "sober thought" at a time. I am no longer a slave to my weaknesses but I am an overcomer.

Thoughts lead to words, words lead to action, and action leads to victory. Whether this is day one or day 3001, your thoughts matter. You have the power to change your thoughts and eventually your thoughts change you. I encourage you to take stock and get rid of "stinking thinking". Be encouraged to rise above your self-imposed limits. Allow these ninety sober thoughts to help you examine and recreate your own thoughts. Don't get so hung up on perfection but rather on progression. You are an amazing work in progress!

TAKING FLIGHT!

Recovery is a journey, not a destination!

I boarded this plane to begin my journey in the "State of Confusion," in the "City of Uncertainty." The flight attendant *(my sponsor)* advised me to buckle up and lock my seat tray in the upright position, because on this journey there would be some turbulence. In case of an emergency, an oxygen mask *(12 steps)* would drop down in front of me. I would need to first place the mask on myself so that I may help another alcoholic.

The journey to recovery in the "City of Serenity" is a direct flight that I must take "one day at a time." In case of an emergency set-back, I should use my Higher Power and the fellowship as a floatation device to get me back to a safe place. Looking out from my window, I will not regret my past and I will see pink clouds and 12 promises. The further I travel along this journey; the miracles will reveal themselves.

My flight attendant has several suggested reading materials, and the onboard movie features myself and others that share experiences, strengths and hopes. Although it might be a long journey, there is a silver lining in every cloud and a pot of gold at the end of the rainbow. I will have family and friends looking forward to the new me that will be born after each daily reprieve.

SOBER THOUGHT #1

On April 7, 2018, enough was enough! I was tired of the struggle, tired of "being sick and tired," and tired of being the person I had become. What started out as "a party over here, party over there" turned into an everyday thing. I considered myself a situational drinker; whatever the situation was, I drank. I was spending all my time and money looking for an escape. What I needed was an escape from the bondage of drinking.

Hennessy *($50 a bottle)* was my number one choice, and I chose it often. For my 50th birthday, friends and family gifted me with lots of bottles, but they didn't last long. The more I had, the more I drank. Every day at 6 pm, my drinking would start, and I never knew what drunken stupor shenanigans would occur. A sobering moment happened when I caught a glimpse of myself on my home security camera. I saw my undesirable behavior and I saw the hell I was living through and putting my loved ones through.

On April 7, 2018, I attended my first recovery meeting with my wife. I had been through a recent successful weight loss journey, so I understood the power of a support meeting. However, I learned the importance of progress, not perfection. The only way to truly overcome is to take the steps. One day at a time leads to one chip at a time; leads to milestones and anniversaries.

As recovery is ongoing, I know that we need each other to survive. The beauty is that we all start at rock bottom and grow up through the process. Now that I have changed my thinking and changed my ways, my mission is to share my sober thoughts to help others on the journey.

HELLO...

My name is Kevin, I was the problem, and alcohol was the pollution, not the solution.

What is your name?

_____

Who are you?

_____

_____

_____

_____

_____

_____

_____

_____

_____

_____

_____

_____

_____

_____

SOBER THOUGHT #2

Selfie-Do You Like Who You See?
The world sees you, the you that you portray
The you of today, not yesterday or tomorrow
They don't see the path of sorrow
No real happiness or bliss
Not the real Mr. or Miss
Only you see you because the third eye doesn't lie
Material things don't matter
As a matter of fact
At any time God can take them back
What's in your heart is the truth
As funny as it seems
What really defines you are
Your true hopes and dreams
When you were an innocent boy or girl
You dreamed you would conquer or save the world
That you would marry the perfect boy or girl
Be rich, not poor
Not hated, but adored
But life happens, not by happenstance
You take some risks, you play it safe
You take a chance
You quickly learned how to do the dance
To the beat of this harsh drum of life
Yes, this life thing is hard
It's complex yet it can be simple
Keep it simple stupid; or are you stupid simple
These words reflect on the real me
The selfish, selfless true selfie
Then I asked, "Do I like or respect what I see?"

What does your "selfie" look like?

_____

_____

_____

_____

_____

_____

_____

_____

What do you want your "selfie" to look like?

_____

_____

_____

_____

_____

_____

_____

_____

SOBER THOUGHT #3

There is no such thing as "impossible;" but rather, "I'm Possible" because of Him.

How has your "impossible" become possible?

_____

_____

_____

_____

_____

_____

_____

What do you now believe?

_____

_____

_____

_____

_____

_____

_____

SOBER THOUGHT #4

Sober Rights

1. You have the right to remain sober.
2. Anything that you said or did in the past you will no longer hold against yourself.
3. You have the right to assume a new sober identity and to make amends for past mistakes.
4. You have the right and privilege to let go of the person who misrepresented your true self.
5. You have the right to live freely.

What rights have you given up in the past?

_____

_____

_____

_____

_____

_____

How will reclaiming those rights change your life?

_____

_____

_____

_____

_____

SOBER THOUGHT #5

Don't remain a victim but celebrate the victory of survival. You were created in God's image. That is the beginning of your victory.

Draw an image that represents where you are on your journey.

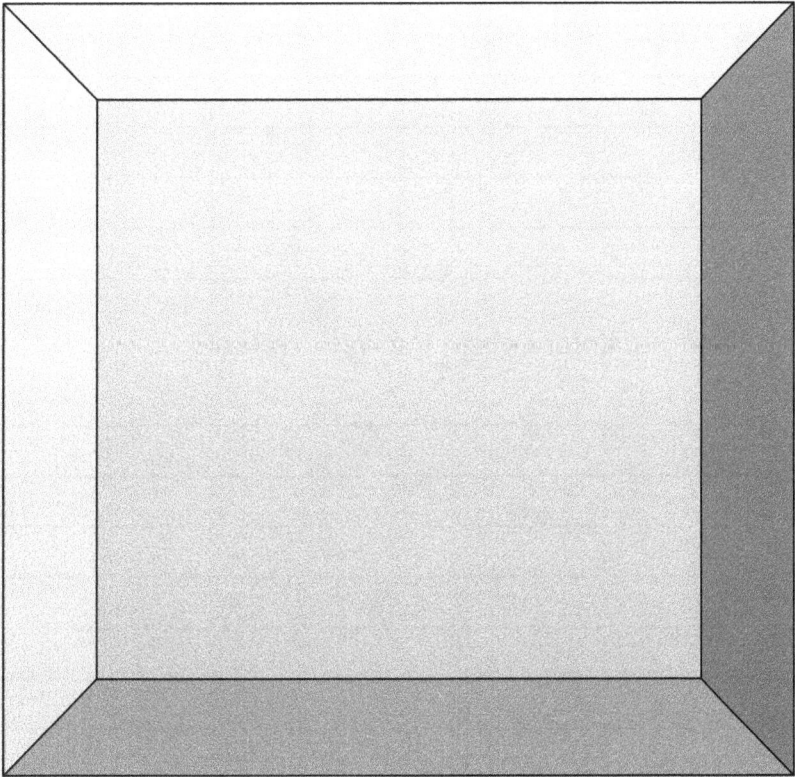

SOBER THOUGHT #6

The journey must start one step at a time; one day at a time; one pound at a time; one dollar at a time. It is not a resolution but evolution.

How do you feel right now?

_____

_____

_____

_____

_____

_____

_____

What is different about the way you feel?

_____

_____

_____

_____

_____

_____

_____

_____

_____

SOBER THOUGHT #7

Consider it a privilege to be right where you are, doing precisely what you are doing. Then you will find opportunities or opportunities will find you for true fulfillment.

What new opportunities have you discovered?

_____

_____

_____

_____

_____

_____

_____

What do you think will bring you true fulfillment?

_____

_____

_____

_____

_____

_____

_____

SOBER THOUGHT #8

Be sure to start at the beginning; follow through the middle, and stop at the end. Many people feel that they can take shortcuts, or skip steps, then do extra credit afterward to make up for what they messed up. Two after one, and three after two; order and borders matter!

What is the first thing that you need to do?

_____

_____

_____

_____

_____

_____

What's next?

_____

_____

_____

_____

_____

_____

_____

SOBER THOUGHT #9

What is the **T.R.U.T.H.**? The **R**eal **U** **T**otally **H**onest. We must be honest in all our affairs because only the truth will set you free.

What has been the best **T.R.U.T.H.** that you have

discovered or revealed about yourself?

_____

_____

_____

_____

_____

_____

What are you afraid to reveal?

_____

_____

_____

_____

_____

_____

_____

SOBER THOUGHT #10

Yesterday's experiences, support today's lessons, which enhance tomorrow's goals and lead to the future you desire.

What are the biggest lessons you have learned from past experiences?

_____

_____

_____

_____

_____

_____

_____

Now what...

_____

_____

_____

_____

_____

_____

SOBER THOUGHT #11

Lord, thanks for the lessons taught, and the lessons learned. Thanks for the things I remembered and the terrible things I forgot. Thanks for money saved and money spent. Thanks for the loves gained and yes, the loves lost. Thanks for today and for many more tomorrows. Thanks Lord for making me in your own image. Thanks for being my father.

What are you thankful for?

_____

_____

_____

_____

_____

_____

What is one lesson learned that has been life-changing?

_____

_____

_____

_____

_____

_____

SOBER THOUGHT #12

Stop thinking that you can't and start knowing that you can. If you can conceive it, then you should believe it.

What do you believe about yourself?

_____

_____

_____

_____

_____

_____

_____

How does that match your actions?

_____

_____

_____

_____

_____

_____

_____

_____

_____

_____

SOBER THOUGHT #13

It is better to fail at complete success than succeed at complete failure. God knows your strengths and wants you to strengthen your weaknesses.

My strengths are…

_____

_____

_____

_____

_____

_____

_____

_____

My areas for improvement are…

_____

_____

_____

_____

_____

_____

_____

_____

SOBER THOUGHT #14

Talk is cheap but action is priceless. Don't talk about it, be about it.

What is the big thing you have been talking about doing?

_____

_____

_____

_____

_____

_____

_____

What is the next action you will take to do it?

_____

_____

_____

_____

_____

_____

_____

_____

_____

SOBER THOUGHT #15

Close your eyes so you might see.
Open your heart so you can love.
Close your doors to temptation.
Open your mind to the possibilities.
Prayer changes things…and people.

Write a prayer that expresses your desire for change.

_____

_____

_____

_____

_____

_____

_____

_____

_____

_____

_____

_____

_____

_____

SOBER THOUGHT #16

Don't ask yourself if you can do it. Ask yourself how you can do it. Then remind yourself why you want to do it. Imagine how good it will feel when you have achieved whatever it is you wish to achieve. The saying is, "Make it do what it do;" not could do or wish it could do. Try or do something you have never tried or done, and you will accomplish something you have never accomplished.

The thing I want to try is…

_____

_____

_____

_____

_____

_____

My "why" is…

_____

_____

_____

_____

_____

_____

SOBER THOUGHT #17

Sober thoughts lead to positive actions that lead to positive results.

How do you need to redirect your thoughts?

_____

_____

_____

_____

_____

_____

_____

How will that impact your results?

_____

_____

_____

_____

_____

_____

_____

SOBER THOUGHT #18

Two things to add to your daily exercise routine: a chance and a choice.

What choices do you need to change?

_____

_____

_____

_____

_____

_____

_____

What chances do you need to take?

_____

_____

_____

_____

_____

_____

_____

SOBER THOUGHT #19

On this journey, you will travel from a State of Confusion to the City of Serenity.

What is the most amazing thing that you have discovered on your journey thus far?

_____

_____

_____

_____

_____

_____

_____

_____

Write down the names of the most influential people on your journey thus far.

_____

_____

_____

_____

_____

_____

SOBER THOUGHT #20

Think ahead, act ahead and you will get ahead.

What thinking adjustments are necessary for you to get ahead?

_____

_____

_____

_____

_____

_____

What actions need adjustments for you to get ahead?

_____

_____

_____

_____

_____

_____

_____

_____

SOBER THOUGHT #21

Whether you are ninety-five years old, fifty-five years old, forty-five years of age, or five, you have the exact same amount of time available to you. Everyone only has this moment to live. For all, there are sixty seconds in a minute; sixty minutes in an hour; twenty-four hours in a day; seven days in a week, and 365 days in a year. Every minute should focus on the good of that moment.

How have you been wasting time?

_____

_____

_____

_____

_____

_____

How can you use your time more wisely?

_____

_____

_____

_____

_____

_____

SOBER THOUGHT #22

Lord, I know that I am not perfect, but each day I strive to be at least better than the day before. I strive to provide a better life for my family. It has been said that life is 10% of what happens to you and 90% of how you handle it. You only live once, so enjoy each day as if it was your last.

If this was truly your last day, what would be the most important thing for you to do today?

_____

_____

_____

_____

_____

_____

What is on your list of things to do today?

_____

_____

_____

_____

_____

_____

_____

SOBER THOUGHT #23

Children are not perfect. Your friends are not perfect. Your family members are not perfect. Your job is not perfect. Your mate is not perfect. YOU ARE NOT PERFECT. Let's not waste more time complaining about the things we said "are not perfect" and enjoy those things that are the good choices that we have made. We were made in His image and that is good!

Since you were made in His image, make a list of the good things about yourself:

_____

_____

_____

_____

_____

_____

_____

_____

_____

_____

Next to each item, write the word, **"GOOD"**.

SOBER THOUGHT #24

Don't deny who you are to attempt to be who you are not.

Who have you been pretending to be?

_____

_____

_____

_____

_____

_____

_____

_____

Why have you been denying your true self?

_____

_____

_____

_____

_____

_____

_____

_____

SOBER THOUGHT #25

There is only one who is higher
There is only one who is greater
There is only one who has ALL power
There is only one who has ALL the love

I call him Lord
I call him Jesus
I call him God
He calls me chosen
He calls me His own
He calls me friend
He calls me forgiven
He calls me loved

How do you identify your higher power?

_____

_____

_____

_____

Who are you to your higher power?

_____

_____

_____

_____

SOBER THOUGHT #26

You have the power to forgive. You have the power to appreciate. You have the power to express yourself and you have the power to listen. You have the power to teach, and you have the power to learn. You have the power to look at a problem and to find within it a positive opportunity. You have the power to see what's wrong with a situation and to take the steps that will make it right. When you let others affect you, then you relinquish that power. If you allow a salary to define you, then you give up the power. If you let society set your limits, then you give them the power. God gives you the power to make choices in your life. Give the glory to God, for that is who really has all THE POWER.

What power do you need to take back?

_____

_____

_____

_____

What is the first step you will take?

_____

_____

_____

_____

SOBER THOUGHT #27

It is not who you know, it is about who knows you. It is not about how much you make; it is about how much you keep. It is not about who you love, it is about who loves you. I know Jesus loves me and He loves you no matter what you have done or left undone.

In what ways do you feel God's love for you?

_____

_____

_____

_____

_____

_____

_____

_____

In what ways can you show more of God's love to others?

_____

_____

_____

_____

SOBER THOUGHT #28

To have breadcrumbs, you must first have bread. If you believe that all life has to offer you is just crumbs, then you have failed to see the loaf of bread from which it came. Always see the bigger picture.

How have you settled for crumbs?

_____

_____

_____

_____

_____

_____

_____

What does the whole loaf look like to you?

_____

_____

_____

_____

_____

_____

_____

SOBER THOUGHT #29

Showing love to others brings love. Showing respect to others brings respect. It is easier to show love and respect for others when you first love and respect yourself.

In what ways have you been unloving and disrespectful to yourself?

_____

_____

_____

_____

_____

_____

_____

_____

What adjustments do you need to make?

_____

_____

_____

_____

_____

_____

SOBER THOUGHT # 30

Write down your reflection of the past 30 days.

_____

_____

_____

_____

_____

_____

_____

_____

_____

_____

_____

_____

_____

_____

_____

_____

_____

_____

SOBER THOUGHT # 31

Show yourself some grace because the best "you" is yet to come. "He who has begun a good work in you will complete it until the day of Jesus Christ." Philippians 1:6

How can you show yourself more grace?

_____

_____

_____

_____

_____

_____

_____

How can you show more grace to others?

_____

_____

_____

_____

_____

_____

SOBER THOUGHT #32

Q: When does one need to be loved? **A:** When you are at your lowest point. **Q:** When does one need to be respected? **A:** When you give respect. **Q:** When does one need to be truthful? **A:** When you are asked a question. **Q:** When does one need to do their best? **A:** When one is faced with a challenge. **Q:** When does one need to give up? **A:** NEVER!

What do you need most in your life right now?

_____

_____

_____

_____

_____

_____

What are you tempted to give up on right now?

_____

_____

_____

_____

_____

_____

SOBER THOUGHT #33

If someone is in need; give. If someone is hungry; feed. If someone is down, **lift them up**. If someone is alone, visit. If someone is sick; pray. If someone is ignorant; teach. If you are that someone, give it to the Lord.

What do you need from the Lord right now?

_____

_____

_____

_____

_____

_____

_____

Who needs something from you right now?

_____

_____

_____

_____

_____

_____

_____

SOBER THOUGHT #34

Silence is golden. Communication is platinum. Compromise is priceless. Give a little to gain a lot. Relationships are not 50/50 but rather 100/100. If you only put in fifty percent or half, then you will only reap half the benefits.

Make a list of ten words that can empower your relationships.

1. _____

2. _____

3. _____

4. _____

5. _____

6. _____

7. _____

8. _____

9. _____

10. _____

SOBER THOUGHT #35

When you stop loving, you cease truly living. When you embrace hate, you embrace death. Keep loving and living.

What seeds of love and life do you need to sow today?

_____

_____

_____

_____

_____

_____

_____

What hatred do you need to let go of today?

_____

_____

_____

_____

_____

_____

_____

SOBER THOUGHT #36

Some people want to make you feel bad so they
can feel better.
Some people might laugh at you because they cry
about themselves.
Some people might hate you because they feel
unloved.
Some people put you down because they wish
they could be you.
I fear me; fear yourself
I envy me; envy yourself
I respect me; respect yourself
I admire me; admire yourself
I trust me; trust yourself
I love me; love yourself
Just keep being the best that you can be.

What do you wish that people better understood about
you?

_____

_____

_____

_____

_____

_____

SOBER THOUGHT #37

You never know how far you can go until you take the first step. You will never hit a home run until you take the first swing. You will never succeed until you make an attempt. It has been said that if you fail to plan, then you plan to fail.

How has this been evident in your life?

_____

_____

_____

_____

_____

_____

How do you handle it when things do not go according to your plan?

_____

_____

_____

_____

_____

_____

SOBER THOUGHT #38

Sometimes fear discourages people. However, allow the fear to motivate you to reach beyond your limitations and expand your expectations.

List three fears that have held you back.

1. _____

2. _____

3. _____

How can you reach beyond your limitations?

_____

_____

_____

_____

_____

_____

_____

_____

_____

_____

_____

SOBER THOUGHT #39

If people would recognize and admit to their flaws, then they would be able to enhance their strengths. No one is perfect, we all make mistakes or "miss-takes". We take a fall, take a hit, take a detour, take a chance or take one for the team. Miss "takes" lead to life's lessons, that lead to victories.

Identify one life lesson you learned from your "miss-take"?

_____

_____

_____

_____

_____

_____

_____

How have you applied that life lesson?

_____

_____

_____

_____

_____

_____

SOBER THOUGHT #40

Do situations cause situational drinking, or does situational drinking cause situations?

What situations do you need to stay away from?

_____

_____

_____

_____

_____

_____

_____

What situation has drinking caused that you need to fix?

_____

_____

_____

_____

_____

_____

_____

SOBER THOUGHT #41

It does not matter how much or how little money you have. Each day is not promised, so live and love like each day is the last.

How are you living?

_____

_____

_____

_____

_____

_____

_____

_____

Where is there room for more love?

_____

_____

_____

_____

_____

_____

_____

SOBER THOUGHT #42

Life is about playing the numbers. First impressions should always be good. Second chances should be earned before being given. Three strikes should always be out. Blessings will always come tenfold.

What adjustments would you make if you were given

another opportunity to make a first impression on the 3

important people in your life?

_____

_____

_____

_____

_____

_____

What is the value of a second chance?

_____

_____

_____

_____

_____

_____

SOBER THOUGHT #43

In work, relationships, education and life; shortcuts lead to shortcomings. Don't short circuit your future by taking shortcuts. Press on through the process and master the steps.

Where have you taken shortcuts?

_____

_____

_____

_____

_____

_____

_____

What was the result?

_____

_____

_____

_____

_____

_____

SOBER THOUGHT #44

Just because you think you changed the frame; the picture is the same. Real change happens from the inside out, not from the outside, in.

What has been the easiest change to make?

_____

_____

_____

_____

_____

_____

What has been the most challenging?

_____

_____

_____

_____

_____

_____

_____

SOBER THOUGHT #45

You are a better person when you recognize that you can be a better person.

What is one thing that you believe makes you a better person?

_____

_____

_____

_____

_____

_____

_____

_____

How did you achieve that or how will you accomplish that?

_____

_____

_____

_____

_____

_____

SOBER THOUGHT #46

To be powerful, you must have power. To be beautiful, you must have beauty. To be faithful, you must have faith.

What do you believe makes you powerful?

_____

_____

_____

_____

_____

_____

_____

What is the connection between faith and power?

_____

_____

_____

_____

_____

_____

_____

_____

SOBER THOUGHT #47

Half measures avail us nothing. In the culinary world, if you have a recipe and you only use half of an ingredient, the meal won't be as appetizing.

How have you been giving life less than your best?

_____

_____

_____

_____

_____

_____

If so, how would your life be different if you gave a pinch or a spoonful more?

_____

_____

_____

_____

_____

_____

_____

SOBER THOUGHT #48

Just think, things could always be worse. With God on your side, it can only get better.

Make a list of five things that you have overcome since you began your recovery journey?

1. _____

_____

2. _____

_____

3. _____

_____

4. _____

_____

5. _____

_____

SOBER THOUGHT #49

They say there are three types of people:
Those that know and know that they know.
Those that don't know and know that they don't know.
Those that think that they know, and don't know that they don't know.

Which one of these describes your current state?

_____

_____

What do you know now that you wish you knew then?

_____

_____

_____

_____

_____

_____

_____

_____

_____

SOBER THOUGHT #50

On my recovery journey, I put in the necessary work. I agreed to and followed the Standard Operating Procedure (traditions). I committed to the work (the steps) and received the paycheck (the promises). The more work you put in, the bigger the paycheck.

What has been the biggest payoff thus far on your journey?

_____

_____

_____

_____

_____

_____

What future payoff are you looking forward to?

_____

_____

_____

_____

_____

_____

SOBER THOUGHT #51

Keep coming back! *"For where two or three are gathered together in My name, I am there in the midst of them."* Matthew 18:20 NKJV

Write down five things that you value about the fellowship.

1. _____

_____

_____

2. _____

_____

_____

3. _____

_____

_____

4. _____

_____

_____

5. _____

_____

_____

SOBER THOUGHT #52

It's never about your intentions but always about your actions. They say the road to hell is paved with good intentions; however, the road to heaven is paved with good deeds.

What excuses have you allowed to destroy your good intentions?

_____

_____

_____

_____

_____

What good intentions will you turn into actions?

_____

_____

_____

_____

_____

_____

_____

SOBER THOUGHT #53

When life throws you a curveball, you must learn to adjust your swing. Work hard, play hard, pray harder!

How has hard work paid off for you?

_____

_____

_____

_____

_____

_____

_____

What prayers have already been answered?

_____

_____

_____

_____

_____

_____

_____

SOBER THOUGHT #54

It is not about getting high but about going higher. The higher you fly, the flyer you will be.

FLY-Fear-Less You!

How would you rate yourself on the confidence scale 1-5?

Why?

_____

_____

_____

_____

_____

_____

How has your confidence grown thus far on your journey?

_____

_____

_____

_____

_____

_____

_____

_____

SOBER THOUGHT #55

Sometimes fear discourages people. However, fear should inspire you to achieve beyond your own expectations. Once you achieve that goal, reach for an even higher level.

Write down one fear that you overcame to achieve a goal.

_____

_____

_____

_____

_____

_____

_____

How did you do it?

_____

_____

_____

_____

_____

_____

SOBER THOUGHT #56

We are all like diamonds; we start out as "rocks" but the program polishes us into the diamonds that God intended us to be... more shine with no wine!

In what ways do you shine?

_____

_____

_____

_____

_____

_____

_____

How has your shine been enhanced without wine?

_____

_____

_____

_____

_____

_____

_____

_____

SOBER THOUGHT #57

Patience will show progress, which is powerful. Perfection is not possible but the pursuit of it is powerful. It's about progress, not perfection.

How would you rate yourself on the progress scale 1-5?

Why?

_____

_____

_____

_____

_____

_____

What do you consider a 5 and what would it take to reach that?

_____

_____

_____

_____

_____

_____

_____

SOBER THOUGHT #58

To improve your attitude, you don't have to deny reality. When you improve your attitude, it doesn't mean things will be perfect. What it means is that you will be more positive, more effective and more solidly focused on the best possibilities. What it means is that you will live and act from a position of strength.

In what ways have you improved your attitude?

_____

_____

_____

_____

_____

_____

How has that strengthened your position?

_____

_____

_____

_____

_____

_____

_____

SOBER THOUGHT #59

Because I am passive, you may think I am a pushover
Because I am not argumentative, you may think I am arrogant
Because I am intelligent, you may think I am not interesting
That is because you don't know who I am
And you may not be who you want to be

In what ways have you been misunderstood?

_____

_____

_____

_____

_____

_____

How has that impacted your journey?

_____

_____

_____

_____

_____

_____

SOBER THOUGHT #60

Reflect on the past thirty days.

_____

_____

_____

_____

_____

_____

_____

_____

_____

_____

_____

_____

_____

_____

_____

_____

_____

_____

_____

SOBER THOUGHT #61

Beware of the 3 C's: **C**omfortable, **C**areless and **C**aught, which will lead to CONSEQUENCES.

How or with what, have you been comfortable or careless?

_____

_____

_____

_____

_____

_____

Where or how, have you been caught?

_____

_____

_____

_____

_____

_____

_____

_____

SOBER THOUGHT #62

Complacency is a defense mechanism against the fear of success.

In what way have you allowed complacency to hold you back?

_____

_____

_____

_____

_____

_____

How can you turn that around?

_____

_____

_____

_____

_____

_____

_____

SOBER THOUGHT #63

If you practice worry, deception, envy, fear or resentment, you block the power of your own beautiful purpose. Choose to let those things go and allow your life to express your highest values and most treasured dreams. If you let go of the negative, then you reap the possible (your highest values and most treasured dreams). God's promise to His children.

What is stopping you from letting go of negative things in your life?

_____

_____

_____

_____

_____

What is stopping you from letting go of negative people in your life?

_____

_____

_____

_____

_____

_____

SOBER THOUGHT #64

Be faithful, not fearful. Be joyful, not tearful. In life you have choices, so, always choose the good over the bad. Choose up instead of down. Choose right over wrong. Choose faith over fear. Choose life over death.

Make a list of five positive choices that you have made recently.

1. _____

2. _____

3. _____

4. _____

5. _____

How has that made a difference in your life?

_____

_____

_____

_____

_____

_____

_____

SOBER THOUGHT #65

Some people might hate you because they hate themselves. It is impossible to love others when you do not love yourself. It is hard to see the good in others when you do not see the good in yourself. It is hard to believe in others when you do not believe in yourself. Love conquers hate.

What would you say to the haters?

_____

_____

_____

_____

_____

_____

What can you say to yourself to overcome the haters?

_____

_____

_____

_____

_____

_____

_____

SOBER THOUGHT #66

The older you get; you realize that most of your milestones are behind you and all that is left is a bunch of yesterdays and even fewer tomorrows. Respect today because tomorrow is not promised.

What do you want to say to your "yesterday"?

_____

_____

_____

_____

_____

_____

What do you want to say to your "tomorrow"?

_____

_____

_____

_____

_____

_____

_____

SOBER THOUGHT #67

We sleep so we can dream. We dream so we can achieve. We achieve because we believe. Faith in God is the key.

How important to you is it to dream?

_____

_____

_____

_____

_____

_____

In your wildest dreams, what can you imagine achieving?

_____

_____

_____

_____

_____

_____

_____

_____

SOBER THOUGHT #68

Dreams can become a reality, but when haters sleep on us, our realty becomes their nightmare. **Beware of the dream killers.**

Who, besides yourself, has been your dream killer?

_____

_____

_____

_____

_____

How has that impacted your reality?

_____

_____

_____

_____

_____

_____

_____

_____

SOBER THOUGHT #69

Sometimes we get so consumed by making a living that we forget about making a life. Life is made one day at a time, one choice at a time.

Reflect on a choice that you made that made a big difference.

_____

_____

_____

_____

What difference did it make?

_____

_____

_____

_____

_____

_____

_____

_____

_____

SOBER THOUGHT #70

Some people say, "Keep your friends close and your enemies closer," but I say, "Sometimes we can be our own worst enemies" ...and you don't get any closer than that.

What connections/relationships do you need to change?

_____

_____

_____

_____

_____

_____

_____

How will those changes impact your journey?

_____

_____

_____

_____

_____

_____

_____

SOBER THOUGHT #71

Morning time can be considered a mourning time: The light will kill the darkness. This morning was the end of the old beginnings and the start of new endings. Embrace the morning!

What were you in the dark about?

_____

_____

_____

_____

_____

_____

_____

What has the light revealed?

_____

_____

_____

_____

_____

_____

_____

_____

SOBER THOUGHT #72

Time waits for no one. Do not wait another day, do it today!

What do you need to do today?

_____

_____

_____

_____

_____

_____

_____

How will that impact tomorrow?

_____

_____

_____

_____

_____

_____

_____

_____

SOBER THOUGHT #73

You have the power within to do whatever you set your mind to and put in the work to do. *"I can do all things through Christ who strengthens me."* Philippians 4:13 NKJV

In what ways have you doubted God and yourself?

_____

_____

_____

_____

_____

_____

_____

How has that changed?

_____

_____

_____

_____

_____

_____

_____

SOBER THOUGHT #74

When you step your way through life, the heel will be met by a toe. Put some foot in somebody's behind, even if it is your own. Step up, step to it, and keep in step!

What has been the biggest game changer thus far?

_____

_____

_____

_____

_____

_____

How else can you step up your game?

_____

_____

_____

_____

_____

_____

_____

_____

SOBER THOUGHT #75

Make a decision to change your vision. The solution is not in the "solution" (drinks). That solution is mind pollution. The solution is a resolution to avoid the pollution.

How has your vision changed?

_____

_____

_____

_____

_____

_____

What has helped you avoid the "pollution"?

_____

_____

_____

_____

_____

_____

SOBER THOUGHT #76

ASAP-As Soon As Possible

ASAP-Always Say A Prayer

ASAP-After Sobriety A Purpose

What have you discovered about your purpose?

_____

_____

_____

_____

_____

_____

_____

Write a prayer about your purpose.

_____

_____

_____

_____

_____

_____

SOBER THOUGHT #77

Back in the day, the designated driver wasn't necessarily the person that didn't drink; it was the person that was willing to risk getting caught. Once you begin recovery, you become the designated driver, and then it is all about the journey, not the destination.

Where do you see your journey leading you?

_____

_____

_____

_____

_____

_____

What risks do you foresee and are willing to take?

_____

_____

_____

_____

_____

_____

_____

SOBER THOUGHT #78

The only hope I had:

Then:

I hope I make it home safely.

I hope I don't feel sick in the morning.

I hope my credit card goes through.

I hope they don't turn off my utilities.

I hope no one sees the real me.

Now:

HOPE-Help Other People Endure

What do you hope for?

_____

_____

_____

_____

_____

How can you become a HOPE dealer?

_____

_____

_____

_____

_____

_____

SOBER THOUGHT #79

After working the program, I became a THUG...

T.H.U.G.-To Have Unlimited Goals

1. Write down short-term goals.
2. Believe then achieve.
3. Check off the list.
4. "Wash, rinse, repeat."

Make a list of 3 goals to accomplish in the next six months.

1. _____

   _____

2. _____

   _____

3. _____

   _____

Make a list of 3 goals already accomplished.

1. _____

   _____

2. _____

   _____

3. _____

   _____

SOBER THOUGHT #80

The older you get, the more life circumstances you experience. The key is to learn how to deal with your life. Many people say that they are stressed out because they are frustrated from not knowing how to navigate through the circumstances of life. Don't be stressed but be and do your best, because you are blessed.

Make a list of five blessings that you are grateful for.

1. _____

2. _____

3. _____

4. _____

5. _____

Make a list of five ways that you can be a blessing to someone else.

1. _____

2. _____

3. _____

4. _____

5. _____

SOBER THOUGHT #81

The words I use are a choice and can be found in the dictionary. The foods I eat are a preference and can be altered. The children I have were gifts, and they keep on giving. The steps I take are already determined; destiny is God's will.

Make a list of ten powerful words to live by.

1. _____

2. _____

3. _____

4. _____

5. _____

6. _____

7. _____

8. _____

9. _____

10. _____

SOBER THOUGHT #82

Live a B.O.S.S. life!

B.O.S.S.-Better Options Staying Sober

Write down five ways that you can be B.O.S.S.

1. _____
   _____

2. _____
   _____

3. _____
   _____

4. _____
   _____

5. _____
   _____

SOBER THOUGHT #83

When you are on a roll, keep going. When you are in a slump, get going. Get in motion and stay in motion. The possibilities are far more powerful and more numerous when you are taking action.

What "possibilities" do you currently have in motion?

_____

_____

_____

_____

_____

_____

How can you keep that motion going?

_____

_____

_____

_____

_____

_____

SOBER THOUGHT #84

Life has many twists and turns, but the road to recovery is a direct route to your destiny…Turn on your GPS and allow him to take you there.

GPS-God Protects Sobriety

Reflect on the ways you have been protected.

_____

_____

_____

_____

_____

_____

_____

Write a prayer for protection.

_____

_____

_____

_____

_____

_____

_____

SOBER THOUGHT #85

In life, some people are participators and others are spectators. The choice is yours!

What are you leaving in the past as a spectator?

_____

_____

_____

_____

_____

_____

What does your future look like as a "participator"?

_____

_____

_____

_____

_____

_____

_____

SOBER THOUGHT #86

Honor how you live so people don't have to mourn how you died.

What is your reason for living?

_____

_____

_____

_____

_____

_____

_____

What is on your "bucket list"?

_____

_____

_____

_____

_____

_____

_____

SOBER THOUGHT #87

Wherever you are, you don't have to stay there.
Wherever you are, you can go further.
Wherever you want to go, God can take you there.

Think about how far you have come. Where do you see

God taking you?

_____

_____

_____

_____

_____

What will it take to get there?

_____

_____

_____

_____

_____

_____

_____

SOBER THOUGHT #88

You might get left behind if you sit on your behind. God wants doers, not just "sayers." You can either talk about it or be about it…the choice is yours!

Make a list of five promises to yourself that you will keep.

I PROMISE…

I PROMISE…

I PROMISE…

I PROMISE…

I PROMISE…

SOBER THOUGHT #89

The end of one thing is the beginning of something else.
Stop regretting endings and start welcoming beginnings.

Write a prayer that welcomes your NEW BEGINNING.

_____

_____

_____

_____

_____

Write five affirmations that celebrate your NEW
BEGINNING!

1. _____

_____

2. _____

_____

3. _____

_____

4. _____

_____

5. _____

_____

SOBER THOUGHT #90

Selfie-Do You Like Who You See?
The world sees you, the you that you portray
The you of today, not yesterday or tomorrow
They don't see the path of sorrow
No real happiness or bliss
Not the real Mr. or Miss
Only you see you because the third eye doesn't lie
Material things don't matter
As a matter of fact
At any time God can take them back
What's in your heart is the truth
As funny as it seems
What really defines you are
Your true hopes and dreams
When you were an innocent boy or girl
You dreamed you would conquer or save the world
That you would marry the perfect boy or girl
Be rich, not poor
Not hated, but adored
But life happens not by happenstance
You take some risks; you play it safe
You take a chance
You quickly learned how to do the dance
To the beat of this harsh drum of life
Yes, this life thing is hard
It's complex yet it can be simple
Keep it simple stupid; or are you stupid simple
These words reflect on the real me
The selfish, selfless true selfie
Then I asked, "Do I like or respect what I see?"

What does your "selfie" look like NOW?

_____

_____

_____

_____

_____

_____

_____

Does it look like you want it to look?

_____

_____

_____

_____

_____

_____

_____

_____

_____

_____

Sober Thoughts